SELECTIONS FROM
THE VERY BEST OF
ANDY WILLIAMS

50 60 70 80 90 00 10 20 30

Exclusive Distributors
International Music Publications Limited
Griffin House, 161 Hammersmith Road, London W6 8BS, England

International Music Publications GmbH, Germany
Marstallstraße 8, D-80539 Munchen, Germany

Nuova Carisch S.p.A.
Via Campania, 12 20098 S. Giuliano Milanese (MI)
Zona Industriale Sesto Ulteriano, Italy
20, rue de la Ville-l'Eveque-75008 Paris, France
www.carisch.com

Danmusik
Vognmagergade 7, DK-1120 Copenhagen K, Denmark

Warner/Chappell Music Australia Pty Ltd.
3 Talavera Road, North Ryde, New South Wales 2113, Australia

Folio © 2000 International Music Publications Ltd
Griffin House, 161 Hammersmith Road, London W6 8BS, England

Cover Artwork used by permission from
Sony Music Entertainment (UK) Limited
10 Marlborough Street · London W1V 2LP
www.sonymusic.co.uk

Printed by The Panda Group · Haverhill · Suffolk CB9 8PR · UK
Binding by Haverhill Print Finishers

April In Paris

Words by EY Harburg
Music by Vernon Duke

Butterfly

Words and Music by
Bernie Lowe and Kal Mann

You tell me you love— me, you say you'll be true,— then you fly a-round with some-bod-y new,— but I'm cra-zy a-bout you, you but-ter-

fly. _____ You're treat - in' me mean, you're

mak - in' me cry.___ I've made up my mind___ to tell you good - bye,___ but I'm

no good with - out you, you but - ter - fly. _____ I

knew from the first___ time I kissed you_____ that you were the trou – bl – in'

kind, 'cause the hon – ey drips___ from your sweet lips; One

taste and I'm out___ of my mind. I love you so much, I know

Born Free

Words by Don Black
Music by John Barry

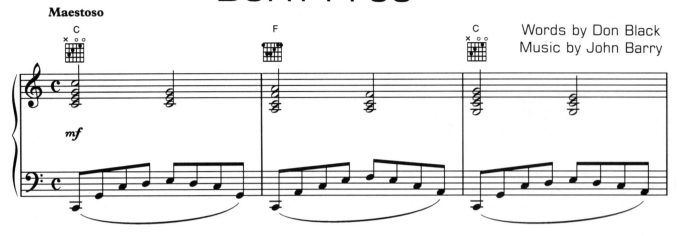

Born free,_____ as free as the
Live free,_____ and beau - ty sur -

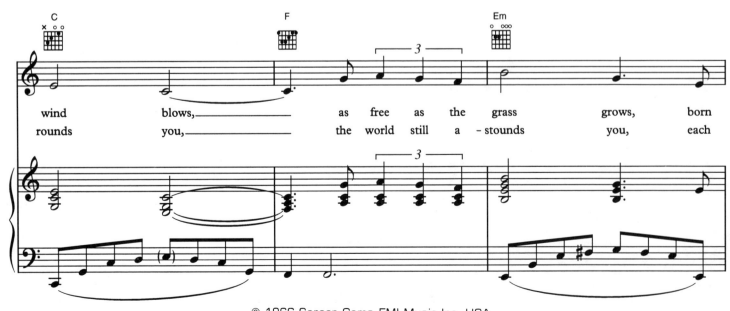

wind blows,_____ as free as the grass grows, born
rounds you,_____ the world still a - stounds you, each

Can't Get Used To Losing You

Words and Music by
Doc Pomus and Mort Shuman

Though it will be emp-ty with-out you._____
Since you're gone it hap-pens ev-'ry day._____
Guess that I am just a hope-less case._____

Can't get used to los-ing you, no

mat-ter what I try to do. Gon-na live my whole life through

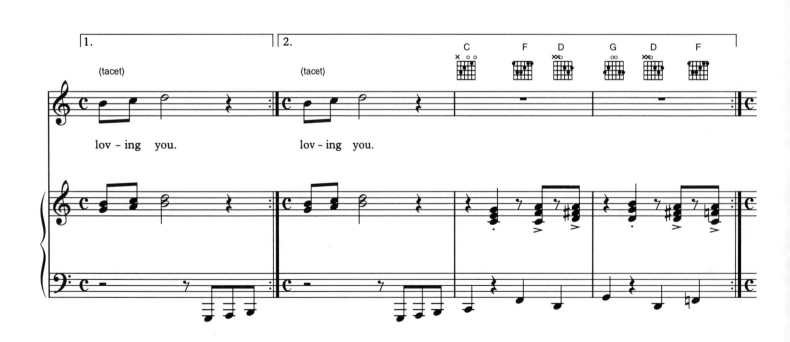

lov-ing you.

lov-ing you.

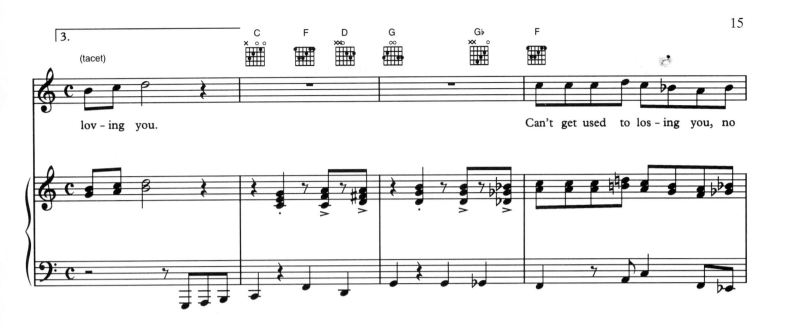

lov - ing you.

Can't get used to los - ing you, no

mat - ter what I try to do. Gon - na live my whole life through

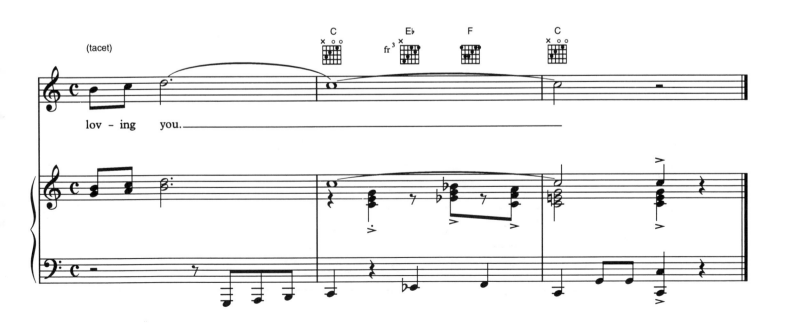

lov - ing you.

Can't Help Falling In Love

Words and Music by
George Weiss, Hugo Peretti
and Luigi Creatore

Lyrics:
Wise men say only fools rush in, _____ but I can't help fall-ing in love with you. Shall I

Can't Take My Eyes Off You

Moderate tempo

Words and Music by
Bob Crewe and Bob
Gaudio

hold you so much, at long last love has ar-rived, and I thank
words left to speak, but if you feel like I feel, please let me

God I'm a-live.
know that it's real. You're just too good to be true, can't take my

eyes off of you. Par-don the eyes off of you.

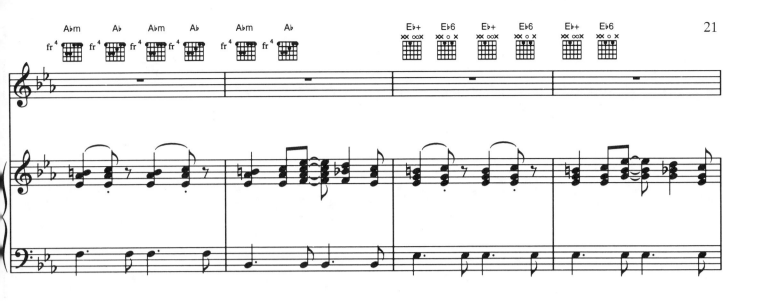

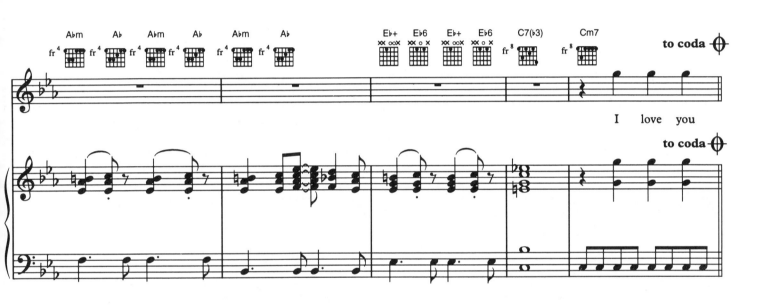

I love you

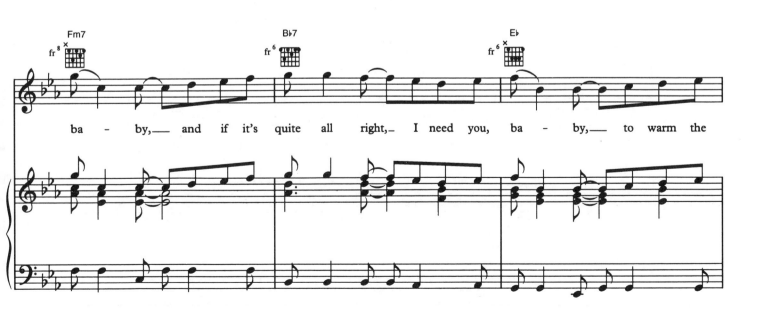

ba - by,— and if it's quite all right,— I need you, ba - by,— to warm the

lone - ly night, I love you, ba - by,— trust in me—when I— say:

Oh pret - ty ba - - by,— don't bring me down, I pray,— oh pret - ty

ba - - by— now that I've found you, stay,— and let me love you,— ba -

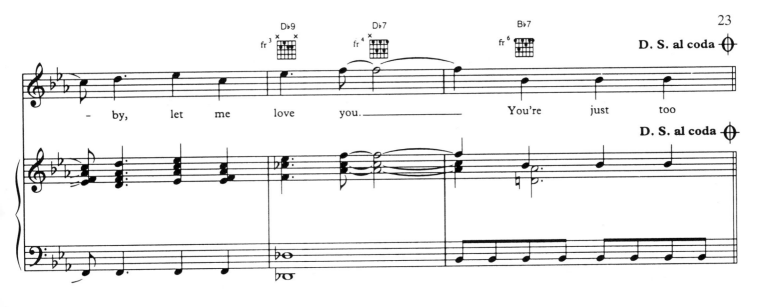

by, let me love you._____ You're just too

D. S. al coda

Coda

ba - by,__ and if it's quite all right, I need you, ba - by,__ to warm the lone-ly night, I love you,

ba - by__ trust in me__ when I say:__ Oh pret - ty

Canadian Sunset

Moderately, with a good beat

Words by Norman Gimbel
Music by Eddie Heyward

Once_____ I was a - lone,
Cold,_____ cold was the wind

so_____ lone - ly and then
warm_____ warm were your lips

Days Of Wine And Roses

Words by Johnny Mercer
Music by Henry Mancini

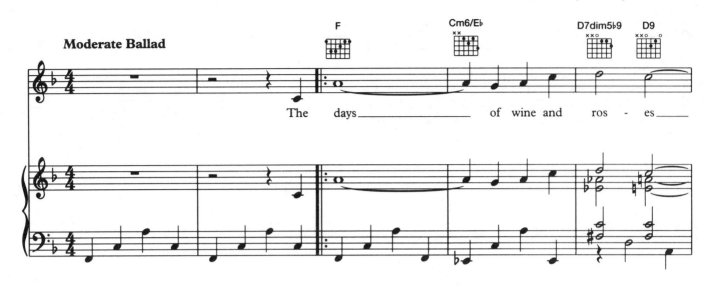

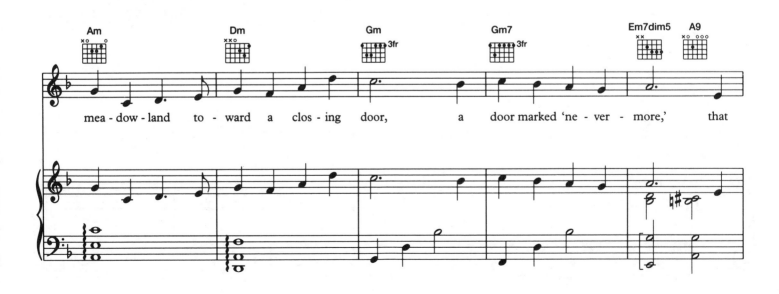

Do You Mind?

Words and Music by
Lionel Bart

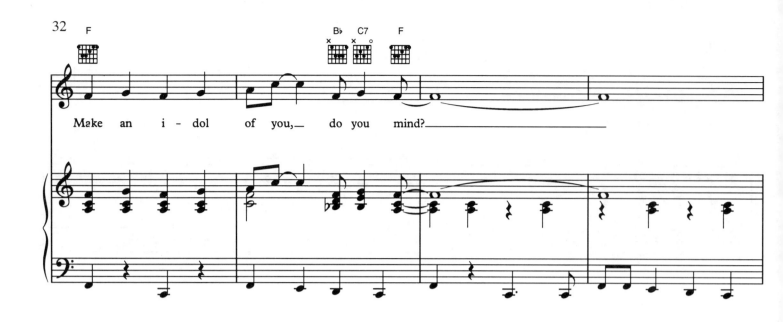

Make an i - dol of you,___ do you mind?___

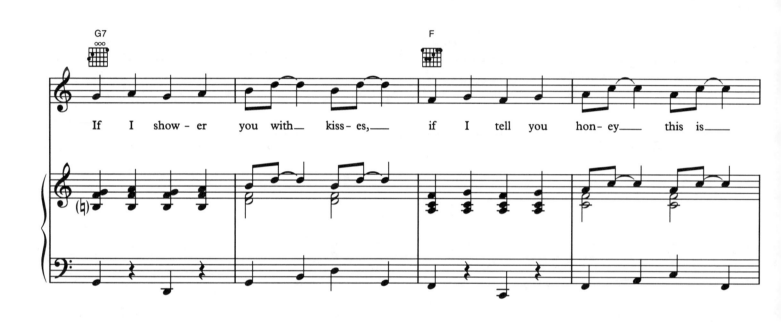

If I show - er you with___ kiss - es,___ if I tell you hon - ey___ this is___

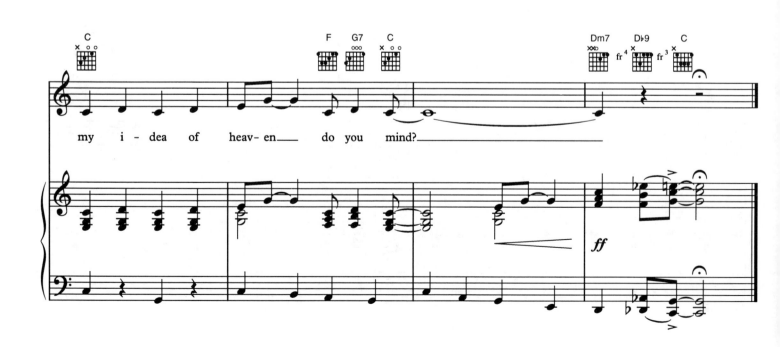

my i - dea of heav - en___ do you mind?___

Dreamsville

Words and Music by
Jay Livingston, Ray Evans
and Henry Mancini

Embraceable You

Music and Lyrics by
George Gershwin and Ira Gershwin

A Fool Never Learns

Words and Music by
Sonny Curtis

Moderately Fast

A fool nev-er learns_ to get a-way, just run a-way, be-

fore his heart be-gins to break;_____ A fool nev-er learns

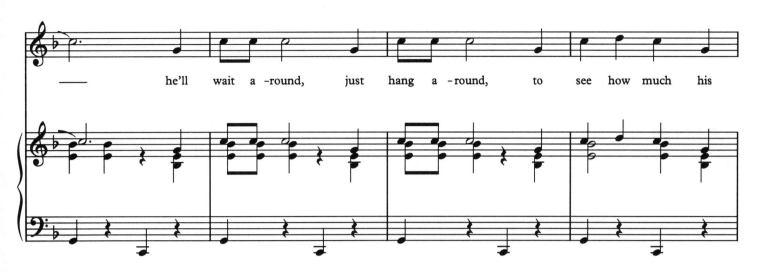

he'll wait a-round, just hang a-round, to see how much his

heart can take._____ A fool nev-er learns_____ to

some girls love is just a game;_____ And some girls treat all

fools the same._____ A fool nev - er learns_____ and I'm

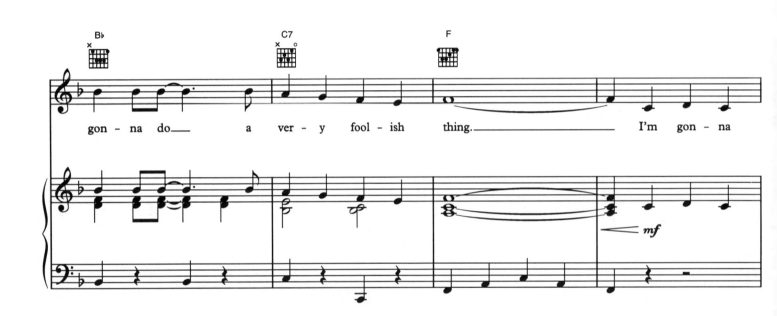

gon - na do__ a ver - y fool - ish thing._____ I'm gon - na

stick by you.____ I'm gon - na hang a -round. Wait a -round.

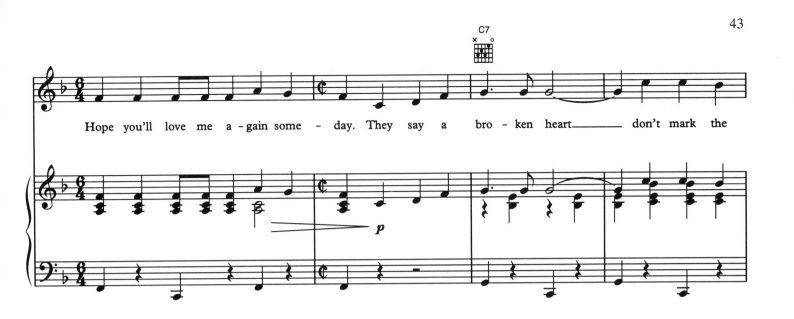

Hope you'll love me a-gain some-day. They say a bro-ken heart_____ don't mark the

end of time._____ That there are lots of girls_____ who'd love to

be just mine._____ But I don't be-lieve_____ that

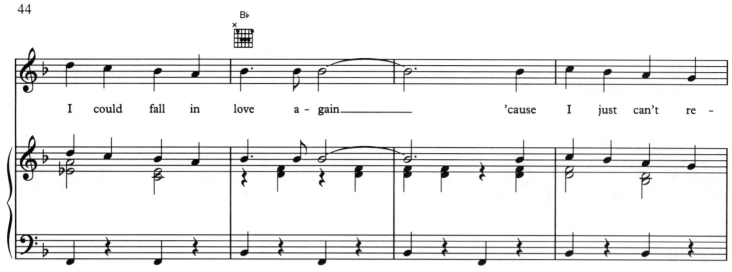

I could fall in love a-gain _____ 'cause I just can't re-

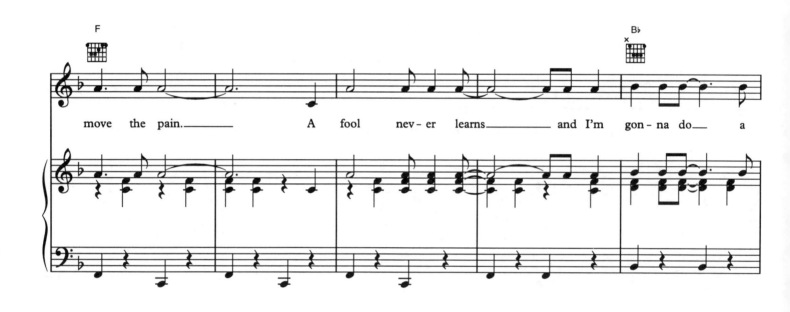

move the pain. _____ A fool nev-er learns _____ and I'm gon-na do ____ a

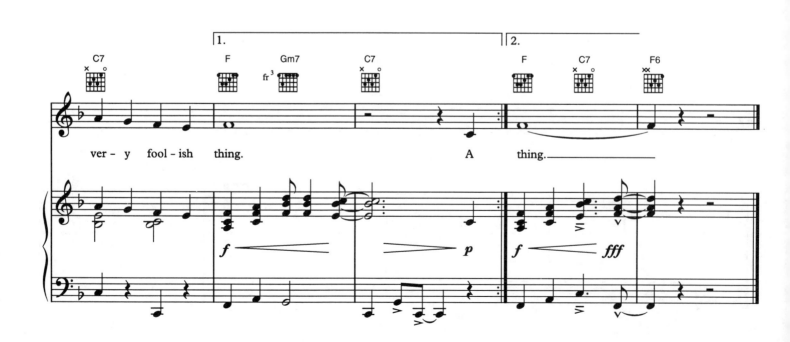

ver-y fool-ish thing.   A   thing. _____

Happy Heart

Words by Jackie Rae
Music by James Last

fi - n'lly will dis - cov - - - er when there is no oth - er for their love.
I've lost all con - trol___ now, I'm not half, I'm whole___ now with your love.

It's my hap - py heart you hear___ sing - ing

loud and sing - ing clear.___ And it's all be - cause you're near___ me, my

love.___ Take my hap - py heart a - way,___ make me

The House Of Bamboo

Words and Music by
Norman Murrells and Bill Crompton

Num-ber fif-ty four,— the house with the bam-boo door,

bam-boo roof and bam-boo walls,— they've ev-en got a bam-boo floor. You must

get to know, So-ho Joe, he runs an
made of sticks, sticks and bricks, but you can

box. I'm a tell- ing you, when you're blue,

well there's a lot to do in the house of bam - boo.

You've got to know,

So - ho Joe he runs an es - pres - so called the

I'm All Smiles

Words and Music by
Herbert Martin and
Michael Leonard

The Impossible Dream

Tempo di Bolero

Words by Joe Darion
Music by Mitch Leigh

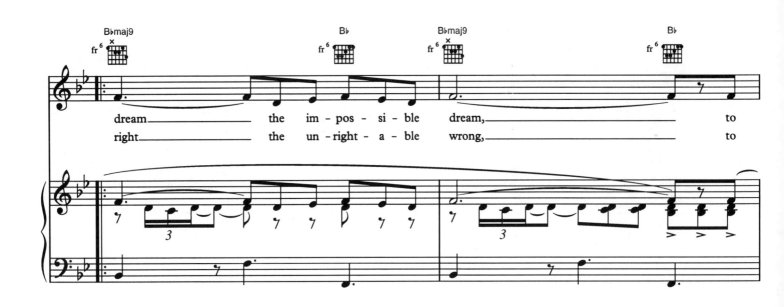

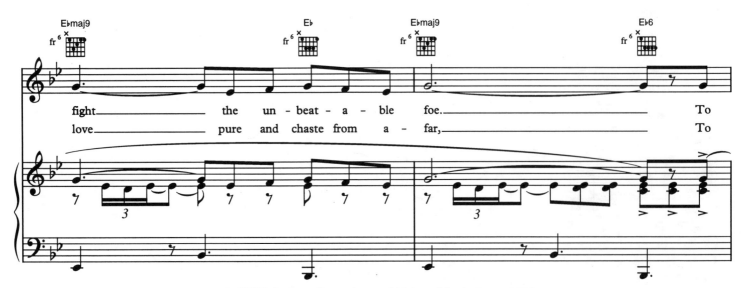

bear_____ with un-bear-a-ble sor-row,_____ to
try_____ when your arms are too wea-ry,_____ to

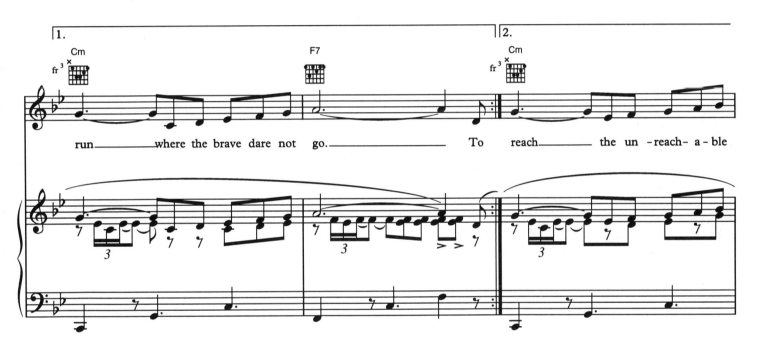

run_____ where the brave dare not go._____ To reach_____ the un-reach-a-ble

star! This is my quest,_____ to fol-low that

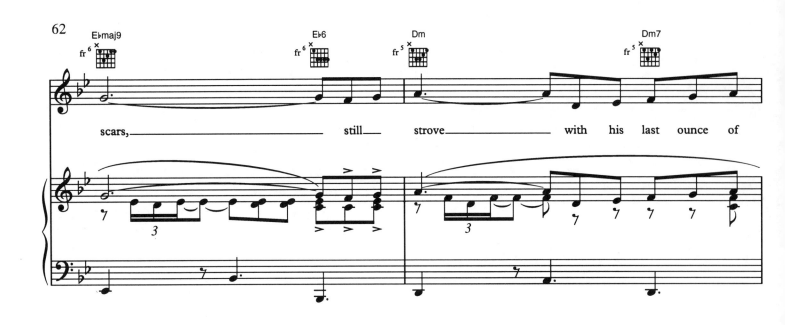

Music To Watch Girls By

Words by Tony Velona
Music by Sid Ramin

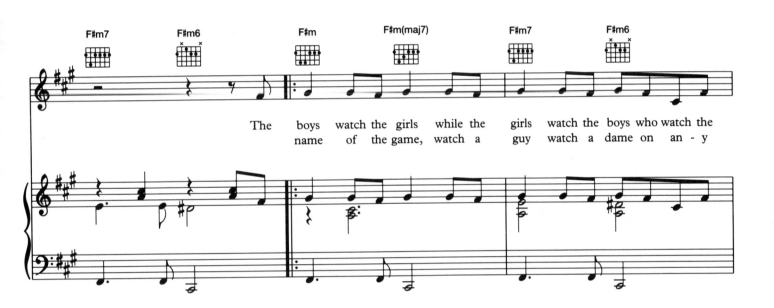

The boys watch the girls while the girls watch the boys who watch the
name of the game, watch a guy watch a dame on an-y

girls go by,___ eye to eye,_ they sol-emn-ly con-
street in town,_ up and down, and ov-er and a-

Watch that sound   each time you hear a   loud   col - lec - tive   sigh

they're mak-ing   mus - ic   to watch girls   by.

In The Arms Of Love

Words and Music by
Jay Livingston, Ray Evans
and Henry Mancini

and share the pro- mise of a new to-

mor - row in the arms of love to - night.

It's So Easy

Words and Music by
David Watkins and Dor Lee

May Each Day

Words by George Wyle
Music by Mort Greene

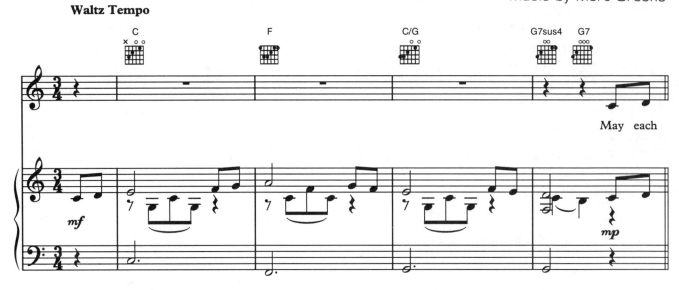

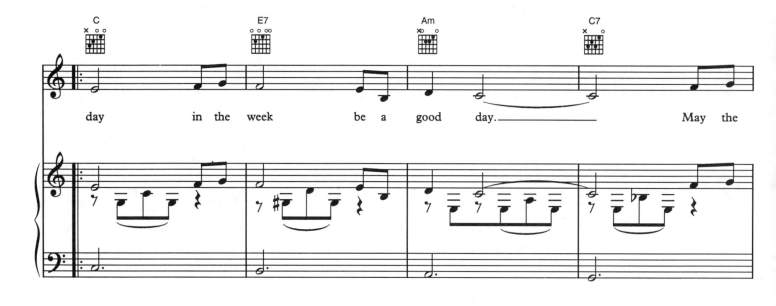

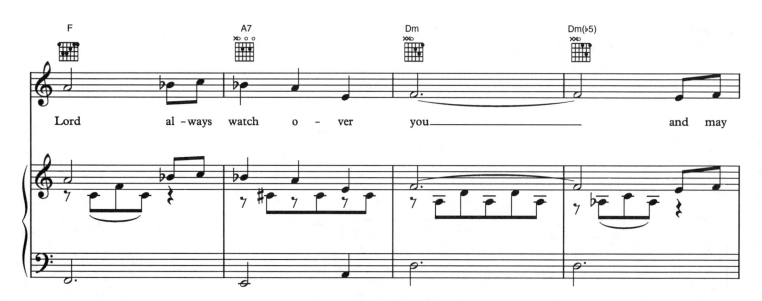

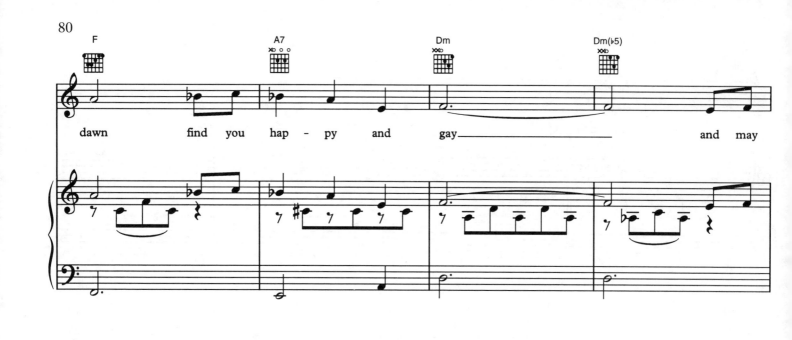

dawn find you hap - py and gay_____ and may

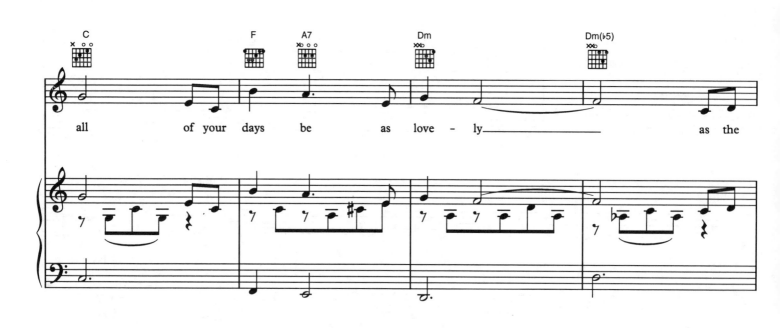

all of your days be as love - ly_____ as the

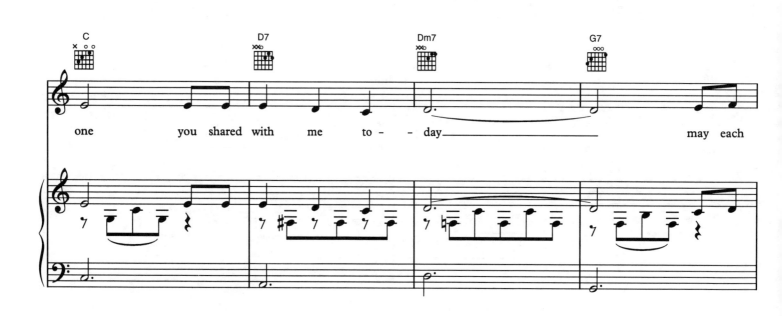

one you shared with me to - day_____ may each

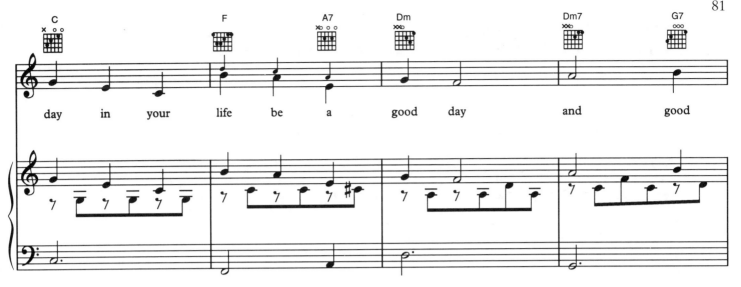

day in your life be a good day and good

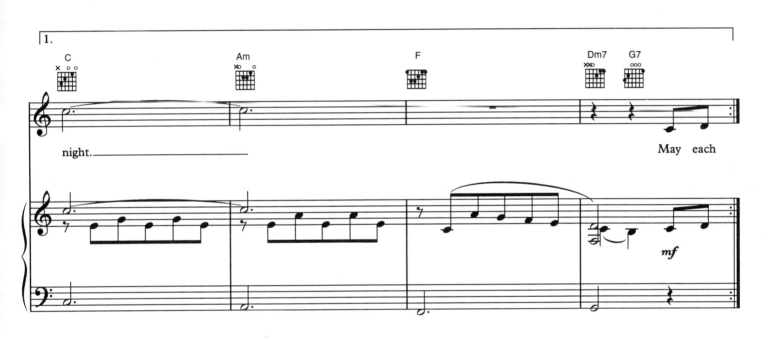

night._____ May each

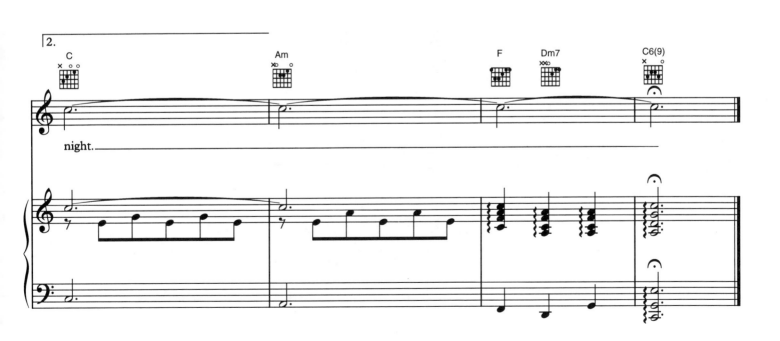

night._____

On The Street Where You Live

Words by Alan Jay Lerner
Music by Frederick Loewe

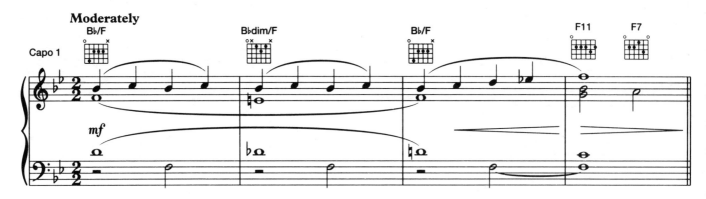

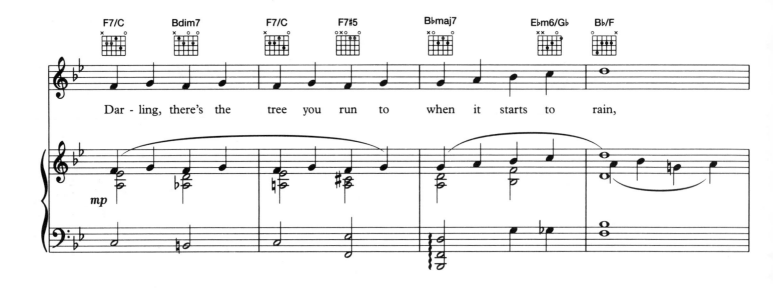

Dar-ling, there's the tree you run to when it starts to rain,

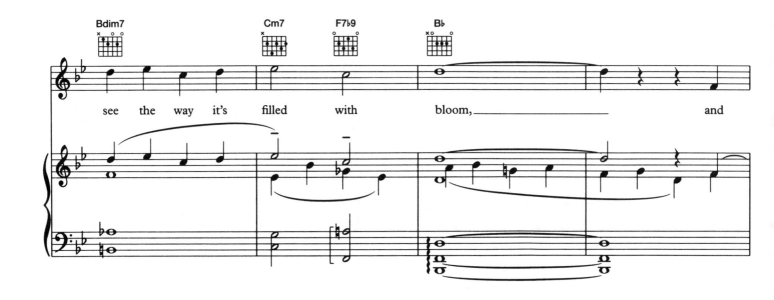

see the way it's filled with bloom,_____ and

The Other Side Of Me

Words and Music by
Neil Sedaka and
Howard Greenfield

September Song

Words by Maxwell Anderson
Music by Kurt Weill

The Shadow Of Your Smile

Words by Paul Francis Webster
Music by Johnny Mandel

Solitaire

Words and Music by
Neil Sedaka and Phil Cody

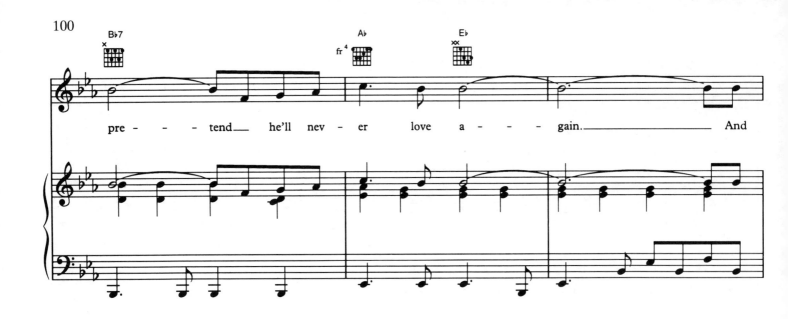

pre - - - tend___ he'll nev - er love a - - - gain.___ And

keep - ing to him - self he plays the game.___ With - out her love it al -ways ends the

same.___ While life goes on a - round him ev - 'ry - where,___ he's play - ing

sol - i - taire._____ _____ And sol - i -taire's the on- ly game in

town,_____ and ev-'ry road that takes him, takes him down.____ While life goes on a - round him ev-'ry-

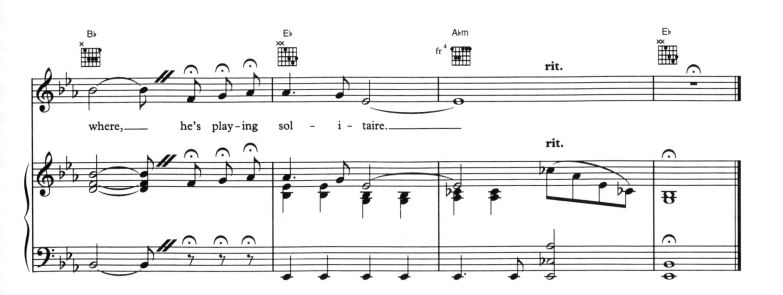

where,____ he's play-ing sol - i - taire._____

Spooky

Words and Music by
Harry Middlebrooks, Mike Shapiro,
Buddy Buie and J R Cobb

1. In the cool of the eve-ning when ev — ery-thing is get-tin' kind of
(2.) al-ways keep me guess-ing and I nev-er seem to know what you are

groo-vy, I call you up and ask you would you
think-ing, and if a fel-la looks at you it's for sure

Let's dance.

If you de - cide — to may-be stop this lit - tle game that you are play-ing, I'm

gon - na tell you all —— that my heart has been dy - ing to be say - ing,

Up, Up And Away

Words and Music by
Jim Webb

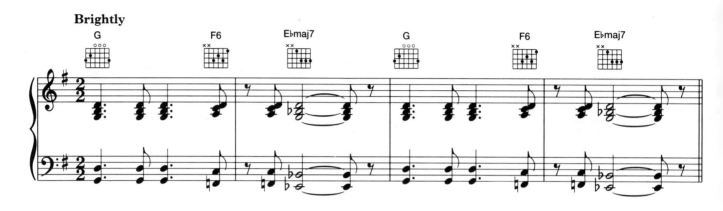

Would you like___ to ride___ in my___ beau - ti - ful___ bal - loon?
world's a ni - cer place___ in my___ beau - ti - ful___ bal - loon,
Love is wait - ing there___ in my___ beau - ti - ful___ bal - loon,

Would you like___ to glide___ in my___ beau - ti - ful___ bal - loon?
it wears a ni - cer face___ in my___ beau - ti - ful___ bal - loon.
way up in___ the air___ in my___ beau - ti - ful___ bal - loon.

The Village Of St Bernadette

Words and Music by
Eula Parker

Stranger On The Shore

Words by Robert Mellin
Music by Acker Bilk

Moderato (with feeling)

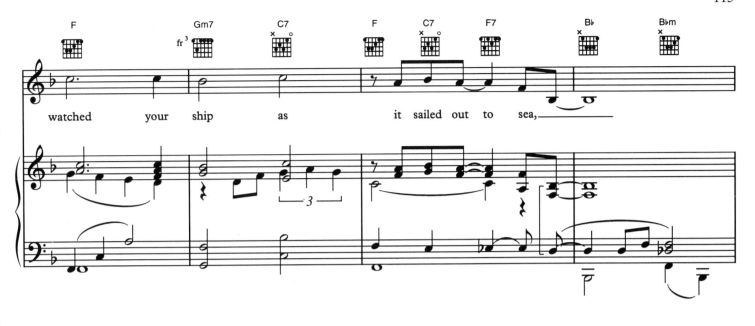

watched your ship as it sailed out to sea,_____

tak - ing all___ my dreams and tak - ing all___ of me.___

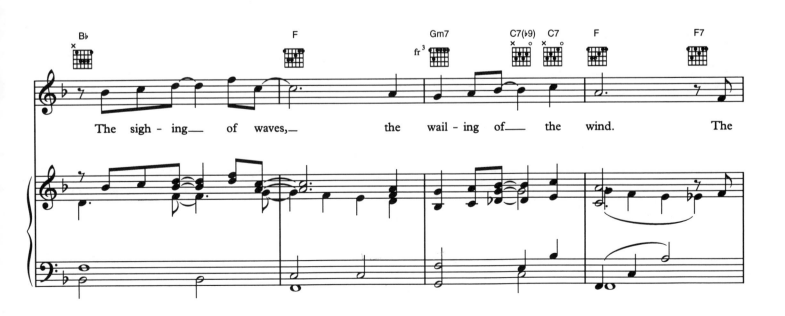

The sigh - ing___ of waves,___ the wail - ing of___ the wind. The

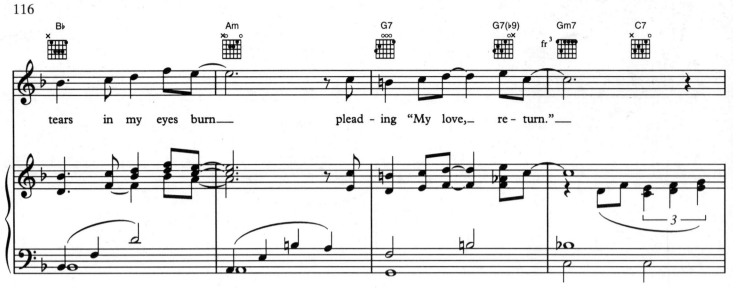

tears in my eyes burn___ plead-ing "My love,___ re-turn."___

Why oh why must I go on___ like this?___ Shall I just be___ a

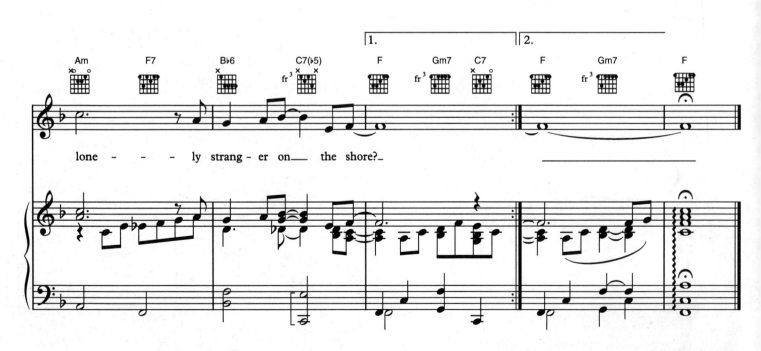

lone - - -ly strang-er on___ the shore?___

Printed in England
The Panda Group · Haverhill · Suffolk · 3/00